THOUGHT TALK

COMMUNICATING WITH THE WHOLE PERSON:
SPIRIT, MIND, AND BODY FOR OPTIMAL POSITIVITY

C. RAY COLLINS

Copyright © 2020 by C. Ray Collins

THOUGHT TALK

All rights reserved. No part of this publication may be reproduced, distributed, or transmitted in any form or by any means, including photocopying, recording, or other electronic or mechanical methods, without the prior written permission of the publisher, except in the case of brief quotations embodied in critical reviews and certain other noncommercial uses permitted by copyright law. For permission requests, write to the publisher, addressed "Attention: Permissions Coordinator," at info@beyondpublishing.net

Quantity sales special discounts are available on quantity purchases by corporations, associations, and others. For details, contact the publisher at the address above.

Orders by U.S. trade bookstores and wholesalers. Email info@BeyondPublishing.net

The Beyond Publishing Speakers Bureau can bring authors to your live event. For more information or to book an event contact the Beyond Publishing Speakers Bureau speak@BeyondPublishing.net

The Author can be reached directly at BeyondPublishing.net

Manufactured and printed in the United States of America distributed globally by BeyondPublishing.net

New York | Los Angeles | London | Sydney

ISBN: 978-1-952884-81-8

FOREWORD

Last year, I wrote a book about leadership. In the book, I share how important communication is and how to keep it positive, because positive people create positive work forces, which are more productive. But, after I completed the book and had it published, I realized that this type of positivity is needed everywhere, every day, and all the time.

We need more positivity in our lives. Thus, "Thought Talk" was born. This is the process of communicating with the total person—their mind, body, and spirit. We communicate, not only verbally, but also with expressions, body language, and our subconscious. We want to communicate to the whole person— their mind, their subconscious, their spirit, and their emotions. During that communication, we want to know we are conveying our message, so we need to understand how the subconscious works and what body language can tell us.

If everyone who reads this book practices these simple ways to a more positive life, you will be the Force of Positivity! You can affect ten other people to be positive. Hopefully, they will do the same, and we will create a more positive atmosphere. We will all be in a better place.

"Positive energy puts you in the right place, at the right time. You'll be amazed at the positive things that will happen to you when you learn to create and maintain high, positive energy levels." --C. Ray Collins

"WORDS"

"Words are pale shadows of forgotten names. As names have power, words have power. Words can light fires in the minds of men. Words can wring tears from the hardest hearts."

--Patrick Rothfuss

CONTENTS

My Story: *09*

Chapter 1: Communication...*15*

Chapter 2: What We Do...*21*

Chapter 3: What We Say..*31*

Chapter 4: How We Say It...*37*

Chapter 5: What Not to Say..*45*

Chapter 6: Family and Friends...*49*

Chapter 7: Communication Skills......................................*55*

Chapter 8: Body Language..*61*

Chapter 9: Story Speak..*73*

Chapter 10: How We Look..*79*

Chapter 11: Unshakable..*85*

Chapter 12: The Recap..*91*

References and Acknowledgements....................................*98*

Quotes..*99*

MY STORY

As it says on the cover of this book, I was born and raised in rural, southeast Oklahoma. As a young child, I had problem speaking. There were words I couldn't say, and I found myself always searching for alternate words to use, so I didn't have to try and say words I couldn't.

My parents even put me in a speech therapy class to see if it would help, but it didn't. Needless to say, I didn't learn much from phonics, which was taught as take time.

"My Story"

To this day, I don't hear the sounds of some letters the same way most people do, because when I learned to say them, I couldn't pronounce them correctly. The first, second, and third-grades were hard for me. Reading, spelling, and English were my downfalls. In the fourth grade, I started to really have a lot of trouble with my tonsils and had been to the family doctor three or four times.

Remember, I am from rural Oklahoma. We lived about three miles out of our town, which only had about 200 people in it. The school I attended first grade through twelfth grade had less than 200 students, total.

My family doctor was the same one who delivered me. He was located in the county seat, which was less than 4,000 people and about 25 miles from our house. He said I needed to see an ear, nose, and throat doctor (ENT). So, he set up an appointment with the closest one to us—in Paris, Texas—which was big city to me, but it only had about 20,000 people in it.

It was an hour drive for us to get to Paris and see the doctor. He examined me and told my parents I should have my tonsils removed, because they were enlarged and would continue to be a problem for me. My parents agreed and decided to wait about a month before the procedure— for when school would be out for the summer.

Then, the shocker came! The doctor also said, "You know he is partially tongue-tied? I can fix this at the same time I take his tonsils out." My parents couldn't believe it, and I wasn't sure what that meant. I was 11 years old and didn't realize this was my problem with pronouncing my words correctly.

My dad had always thought I was just lazy and didn't try to say words correctly. Even the speech therapist didn't think I was trying hard enough with my pronunciation. But, please remember, I'm from the country—they all did the best they could. But, since I wasn't totally tongue-tied, it was hard to detect without seeing a specialist.

After the surgery, my tongue was swollen as big as my mouth, and I had to drink and eat through a straw for about ten days. Finally, all the swelling was gone, and I was able to eat and speak. One of the words I had never been able to say was "magnificent". I wanted to say it so badly, because I had seen the movie *Magnificent Seven* earlier in that year— yeah, I know I'm telling my age— and had wanted to tell my friends about it, but I couldn't, because I couldn't pronounce it.

This was the test… My mom asked me to say it. I hesitated, but finally, I opened my mouth, and out came "magnificent". I was so happy, and things changed for me. School wasn't as hard. I had never made bad grades, but now, good grades came more easily. Don't get me wrong, I still had— and have— problems with certain words, even to this day. This is mainly because the sounds I learned for certain words were affected by me being tongued-tied, and the words sounded different to me.

Of course, being from the country with a southern accent doesn't help, either. I always thought once I finished my education and moved out into the world, I would lose the accent. But, life always throws you a curveball. The first ten years of my working life, I worked in North Carolina, Georgia, Arkansas, Louisiana, and Texas. Needless to say, the accent is here to stay.

I'm telling you this because I found better ways to communicate with the people around me at a very early age. Even through high school, I was able to communicate well. I was class president a couple of times, FFA president, Most Likely to Succeed, Halloween chairman, and Oklahoma's Outstanding Student.

I graduated high school and started college at East Central University in Oklahoma. I was married, and after my freshman year, I dropped out and started working construction to feed my family. I continued to go college at night, and finally, after several years, I got a degree in business.

I continued to work in the construction industry, but I had been promoted to supervisor. I liked building things and being able to be outdoors and indoors, so I stayed in the industry.

After about eight years, I moved into a management position as a superintendent. As the years went by, I moved up to being a project superintendent, and finally, a senior superintendent— or in some businesses, the construction manager. I was responsible for projects ranging from a few million dollars, to projects of a hundred-million dollars, with work forces going into the hundreds.

About halfway through my 48-year career, I went to work for a construction management company, managing large projects. The last project I managed before I

retired was a $340-million corporate headquarters project. Along with my team, we managed over 70 subcontractors and had our own workforce of about 80 people.

Besides managing the project schedule and budget, we also coordinated the work with all the subcontractors. There were about 12 to 16 supervisors under my direct management, and about the same number of indirect supervisors.

With 40 years of managing people, I have learned a trick or two about leadership and communication. Part of my responsibilities were to help our younger supervisors to improve their own abilities and communication skills.

I came up in the "Old School Style". Construction supervision was considered tough and rough, and their communication skills were just as rough. We told people what to do, and if it wasn't done, we would chew them out—and sometimes, just let them go. However, at an early stage of my career, I learned I could get more out of my team if I treated them with respect and added a little sweetness with it.

Over the years, I continued to educate myself. I took several classes from the Dale Carnegie Institute and attended seminars on communication from people like Nicholas Boothman and Robin Roberts. I read books on psychology and how the subconscious works. I learned that positive communication can be powerful, and talking to the whole person, including their subconscious, was the correct way to communicate. I also realized that using this style helped avoid conflicts and arguments.

The more I learned, the better I became at leading and communicating positively with my teams, and I became very successful. Every project I managed made money, which helped me move up the ladder of management. Many of my team members went on to have very successful careers, themselves—using my style of leadership.

This led me to develop a training to help teach supervisors how to communicate in a positive way that will create a positive workforce that will be more productive. After teaching this course a few times, I realized I wasn't giving a lot of details about the communication styles. I was giving just enough information so they could start putting it into practice. So, I wrote the book *Leadership, Followers, Behavior, and Tools* to be a companion to the training. The tools were something they could start using immediately to create that positive atmosphere. To my surprise, the book became an Amazon best-seller.

As I mentioned earlier, this style of positive communicating would be a benefit for everyone. Let's face it: there are leaders and followers in everything we do—whether it's the family unit, hanging out with your friends, playing a sport, building a relationship, going to church or school, or working with a homeless shelter.

Learning to start the day positively and being able to pass this on to someone else is a great feeling. Seeing the fruit from your positive actions and communicating positively is the most rewarding of anything I have ever done. Once you do see it, you will be driving to start every day in a positive way. You will take steps to ensure you leave your home energized and positive.

The first step starts here: learning about yourself, the subconscious, body language, and the spirit inside of you.

What are we waiting for? I want you to experience the power of positive life and become the force for everyone.

--C. Ray

> *"Welcome every morning with a smile. Look on the new day as another special gift from your Creator, another golden opportunity to complete what you were unable to finish yesterday. Be a self-starter. Let your first hour set the theme of success and positive action that is certain to echo through your entire day. Today will never happen again. Don't waste it with a false start or no start at all. You were not born to fail."* – **Og Mandino**

CHAPTER 1

COMMUNICATION

In this book, we are going to show you how to communicate in a positive way. First, we are going to discuss communication. We are going to give you some of the basics to good, successful communication. Then, we will show you how to be positive, and how to put that into your conversations.

Positivity starts with you. In all you do.

Communication is the key to good relationships—whether you are at work, at home, or just playing. Bad communication has been the problem for as long as man has been communicating. We all are either in a hurry, think it's not important, or assume the other party knows exactly what we are talking about. It doesn't matter which case applies here—what we are not doing is communicating.

There is a story one of my instructors used to help us to learn how easy it is for bad communication to happen, and it goes like this:

A rancher in the northeastern part of Oklahoma was getting ready to start his day. The only help he had was his 13-year-old son. They finished breakfast, and the rancher told his son, "Son, grab the axe, go out to the woods, cut me a ten-foot pole I can stick in between the slats on the fence of the squeeze-chute, so I can stop the cow from going too far backwards."

The son nodded his head and walked out of the house. He stopped at the woodshed and got the axe and started walking towards the woods, which was about a half-mile across the pasture. Later, the farmer was working on his tractor, and his son came carrying about a three-inch diameter pole.

The rancher looked at the boy and said, "Son, you've been gone from almost four hours. Did it take you that long to cut a little three-inch tree?"

The boy replied, "No, sir. When I got to the woods, I didn't know what size to cut to fit in the space between the slates. So, I figured I could cut down approximately a six, four, three, and two-inch tree. After I cut them down, I'm five-foot-four-inches tall, so it was pretty easy to figure how long ten-feet was, and I cut them to size. I carried the six-inch one down to the corral, and it was too big. I walked back to the house and got a measuring tool to measure the space. It was exactly four inches. I walked back to the woods and picked up the one I had cut for the four-inch and brought it back to the corral, but it was slightly too-big also. I didn't have anything to measure the four inches when I cut the poles, so my guess was little big. So, I had to go back to get the three-inch pole, and it worked just fine on the squeeze chute."

The rancher shook his head, told the boy to cut the others into firewood, and he went back to work on the tractor, mumbling to himself, "A simple task, and he makes it complicated."

Here, you have both parties not communicating. The rancher didn't give the son enough information to do the task. He assumed the son knew what to do, and the son didn't ask any questions—probably because he wanted to hurry and to please his dad, or he just thought he knew what to do.

How many times has this type of scenario played out for you? I would bet this has happened with you and your father, or mother, before? I know it has happened with you and one of your friends?

To steal a line from an old movie a lot of you have probably never heard of, but you will probably know the line. The movie was *Cool Hand Luke*. It played in the 60s, and the quote is "What we have here, is the failure to communicate." It was a good movie, and this quote has outlived it.

That "failure to communicate" has happened to all of us. There are really four reasons we have this problem:

1. You're not listening.
2. You don't give enough detail.
3. You're talking over someone's head
4. All the facts are not present.

Not listening is one of the things we do that we don't realize we do. Once the other person says the first sentence or a few words, we start to think about our response, and we don't hear what else they say, or at least not all of it.

We need to train ourselves to listen to all they have to say. Then, take a couple seconds to let your subconscious process and give you options on your response. Be patient, wait, and respond.

By doing this, your response will be more accurate, more detailed, and more acceptable—which means, because you listened and responded to all they had to say, you gave them a moment to think before you responded.

It is easy to train yourself. Be patient and wait for your subconscious.

When I teach about not giving enough details, I like to use the lesson of giving directions to get my point across. So, here's the conversation:

Pam is driving into Ann's hometown to visit her. She has never been there before. She will need to call Ann for directions to her house. She pulls over at a convenience store on Highway 70 and Main Street and gives Ann a call. She tells Ann where she pulled over and asks how to get to her house.

"Pam, it's really easy. Just go towards town four blocks and turn right on Lemon Street. Lemon Street splits off, but stay to the right. Drive until you don't see any houses, then turn on Logan Road. I live on the corner of Logan and Miller Lane about a half-mile down the road. See you when you get here," Ann said and hung up.

It sounds pretty good, but to be driving, and following directions, it's not that good. Let's take a look. The convenience store is located on the far corner of the block. Is she counting this one or four blocks? What's the name of the street that splits off, or is this Lemon? Do I turn just when I don't see houses, or is it a mile up the road to Logan Road? Which way do I turn onto Logan Road? Which corner is Ann's house on—since there's usually four? What's the house number?

It's a good thing that most of us have Google Maps nowadays. The point is, Ann thinks she gave good, simple instructions and was sure Pam understood. She made a couple of common mistakes. She assumed Pam understood, didn't ask any questions to confirm Ann's understanding, nor did she ask if Pam had any questions. Secondly, she didn't give enough details for someone to drive straight to her house.

Even when you are with a friend, details are important in general conversation. I think the most common response in general conversation is "I don't know." Say you are out with a friend, and you have eaten your dinner. You have been seeing the trailers to a couple of new movies, and you would like to see one. You ask your friend, "You want to go to a movie?" Their first response is, "I don't know. What's playing?"

You friend did right by asking for more details, but you could have avoided the need for the questions. You could have started the conversation by saying "I've seen couple good movie trailers, and I think they are shows you would like to see. They are [insert movie titles here]. You want to go?" Now you gave details and maybe your friend can make a decision. If not, they will probably ask a more detailed question.

Whether giving instructions or in general conversations, the key is details, details, and more details. My rule of thumb is to speak and give details as if you are talking to eight to ten-year-old all the time. I know this sounds a little silly, but I would rather be too detailed than not detailed enough and fail to communicate.

We have all done talked over someone's head, or used words or phrases the other party didn't understand. Sometimes, it might be a subject they don't know anything about. If you are the positive force, you don't want to talk over someone's head. Not only are you not communicating, but you could also cause the other person to feel inadequate or dumb.

Be sure to talk in a way that is easy to understand. Sometimes, we assume everyone understands what we say, but the truth is, we talk over their heads or don't give them enough details for them to follow the conversation. Big words are not always necessary, but never assume they know what you are talking about. Be detailed with your instructions. Think about it: how many times has someone said to you, "I didn't know that's what you meant" or "I didn't know that's what you wanted?" In cases like this, poor communication falls on you.

Just because you have three degrees—and one is in English and literature, and you have a very large vocabulary—doesn't mean they help you communicate. You must communicate on the level of the other person. If the other person is talking over your head, let them know you don't understand. Communicating is a two-way conversation.

CHAPTER 2

WHAT WE DO

What we do doesn't have anything to do with other people. It has to do with you. It how we set ourselves up for that positive energy every day. Most people don't think about this, or they don't do enough for your body, mind, and spirit. It is just like getting ready to mow your yard: you check the oil in the mower, fill it up with gas, check what level you want to cut at, and make sure there isn't any trash in the yard before you start.

It's like any task you are going to start— "Get yourself prepared!"

We can't just think that positive energy is going to manifest without a little effort. How many times have you gotten up in the morning and sat around in your pajamas for a couple of hours? Probably several. During that time, how many times did you tell yourself, "I need to get dressed?" Two or three times? Probably. Same goes for making the bed.

Our mind, body, and spirit are talking to us. They are telling us they need more. They need to feel good. They are looking for positive energy. So, you must feed yourself.

Everything starts in your subconscious—your emotions, attitude, and decisions. Your subconscious takes everything in. It processes, analyzes to see if some of it needs to be stored or responded to, and makes you feel good, bad, or sad. If it's good, it releases endorphins, or waves of positive energy. This wave of energy is felt throughout your body.

We want to start the day by creating this wave of positive energy in us, so we can share it with others. The more we share this, the more we will get back and build our wave of positive energy into a surfing wave.

What we do is just as important as what we say, and it starts off in our home, if we are wanting to be a Force of Positivity. It starts with you, and how you start your day.

Please understand that these are suggestions that work for me. Everyone is different and has their own style and order of things they do. You have your own little things that can give you positive energy. I just want to open your mind— your subconscious—to what we do, and how it can set our mood.

My Indian grandpa lived to be 80 years old. He was a good person, but he had a drinking problem— as many did who served in WWII. We lived in very rural Oklahoma, and I used to spend a lot of time with him fishing, hunting, and just hanging out. He lived off his Disability VA check. Every month, he would get his check. He would go pay all of his bills, groceries, gas, electricity, etc. Then, with the money he had left, he would start drinking until all the money was gone, which lasted five to seven days. He would find a way home and stir up some kind of concoction that would make him sick, then to bed he would go for about 20 to 24 hours.

The next day, he would get up and make his bed. Then he would shower, shave, brush his teeth, get dressed, and comb his hair. He did this every day, whether he felt bad or not, of course, but you could tell when he was still wasn't feeling well. I asked why he didn't stay in bed and rest some more.

What he told me has stuck with me all these years, and I practice it every day. He said, "It doesn't matter how bad you feel. Making your bed and getting dressed as if you have somewhere important to go will always make you feel a little better about yourself. If you feel a little better about yourself, others will feel better, too."

Now, back then, it just sounded like good advice, so I started do this. Now, it's just a habit. But what does it really do? It means you done two things that are positive for you. Making your bed is a positive act. Not only have you completed the night, but it also means you are starting your day. Completing a task is positive, no matter how small.

The same goes for getting ready for the day by getting dressed, combing your hair, brushing your teeth, and shaving or putting on makeup. This act is for you. You comb your hair and put makeup on to make you look better, and you do it until you are satisfied—which is a positive act.

This is just some of the actions we do. If we carry these kinds of actions into our day, what happens? We are creating positivity in ourselves that can be picked up by others.

Another simple act is to smile. I'm sure we have all heard the science behind the smile. It sends positive waves to your brain, as well as the people you smile at. Subconsciously, it also causes the other person to want to smile and send more positive waves to their brain and yours.

Just remember, the first smile of the day needs to be to yourself, when you are looking in the mirror, getting ready for the day, so you start the wave of positive energy when you first get up in the morning.

Three little steps: make the bed, get yourself ready for the day, and smile at yourself. These steps have other decisions you will need to make. The choices you make could be positive or negative. What clothes to wear? Wear my hair up or down? Do I need makeup or just base? How about my shoes?

First, most of us think, "I want to be comfortable". That's okay. Just keep in mind, you don't want to wear sweats and a t-shirt to a business meeting just because they are comfortable. So, sometimes, comfort can be negative.

The same can go for the color of your clothes. What color makes you feel good? If you don't like the way brown looks on you, that's a negative. Wear colors that make you feel good. Today, shoes can be almost anything, anytime—from tennis shoes to combat boots to anything in-between. But again, what is proper for what you are doing, and does it make you feel good?

Make sure you are dressing to satisfy yourself and dressing properly for the activity of the day. All of this make will make you feel better. It's positive and sends more waves to your subconscious mind. If you feel better, that positive energy can pass along to another person. Your mood and actions can change their mood and actions—which could then affect someone else.

> *"Positive thinking is powerful thinking. If you want happiness, fulfillment, success, and inner peace, start thinking you have the power to achieve those things. Focus on the bright side of life and expect positive results."* — **Germany Kent**

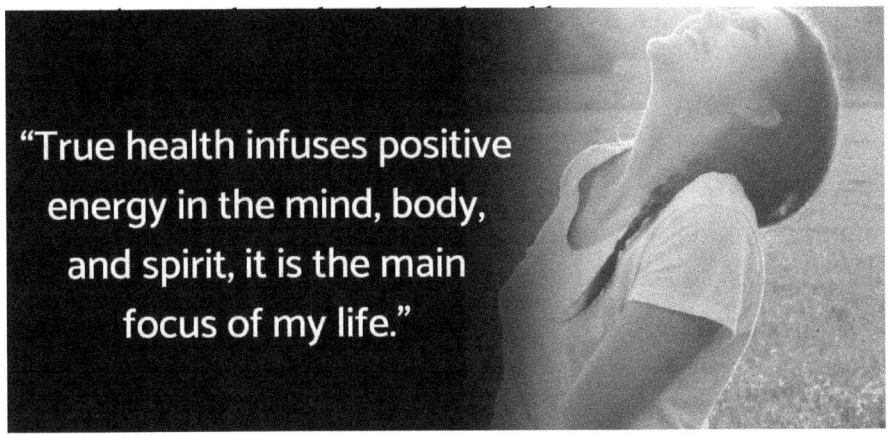

"True health infuses positive energy in the mind, body, and spirit, it is the main focus of my life."

Many years ago, I was having problems focusing. I kept juggling several things at once, but could not seem to keep on any one thing enough to finish. I started taking vitamins that were supposed to help and changed the way I eat. This didn't help much.

One day, while playing golf with my preacher, I mentioned my problem to him, and he gave me the answer. He said, "Look, Claude, you are a positive person, and this is usually not a problem for positive people. Tell me about how you start your day." I explained to him my three steps in the morning: make my bed, get dressed and ready to go, and smile at myself.

He said, "You are only halfway preparing yourself for the day. That's why your mind is wandering. Okay, are you resting well?"

I said, "Yes, I get six to seven hours of sleep most nights."

"Okay," he continued, "are you doing a little exercise and praying in the mornings?"

I said, "No, I exercise two or three times a week, and I pray off and on during the day, but it's not always one of the first things I do."

He said, "Look, here's what you need to do. First, you need a good night's rest. Whatever that means to you. Wake up feeling good. I know you say you work out two to three times a week. That's different than a little, morning exercise. You need to spend about five minutes, every morning, energizing your body. This can be stretches, yoga, pushups, or whatever stimulates your body. Get the blood flowing. It helps to wake up the body. You need this stimulation to connect your brain with your body.

Some of you say, 'Hey, I take a shower in the morning and that stimulates me.' Well, yes and no. It does stimulate you to get ready, to get dressed. It's part of making you feel better, but it's not connecting your mind, body, and spirit," he explained. "Last, you need to meditate or pray. For some folks, meditation works better, but it doesn't matter. Prayer has always worked for me. Not only do I feel closer to God, but I also feel I have cleared out my mind for the day.

After doing all these things, you have completed tasks, talked to your mind, talked to your body, and spiritually refreshed your positive energy. This will not only help to share that energy, but it also keeps you on track. Just give it a try."

Well, he was right. Doing these things changed everything for the better. Not only did I feel better, but I was more positive and focused. Let's talk about these a little more.

Resting means a lot of different things to different people. Like I said, I really feel good on six hours of sleep. If I try and sleep more, I really feel bad. Some may need more or less sleep. Some include a nap in their rest, or just 30 to 45 minutes of quiet time. Do what works for you and makes you feel rested. Feeling well-rested is important. If you wake up tired, or feel you don't have any energy, you are not resting well, or not resting long enough.

You need to find that balance. Maybe you ate too late, or you didn't go to bed when you first felt sleepy. For some, a little stretching before bed may be needed, or maybe you need to shower before bed. Reading helps some clear their mind, so they can rest. Find yours!

Look, it's very simple. Resting is recharging your body and mind. Sometimes, you can rest too much and feel sluggish all day—not just your body, but your mind as well. The right amount of sleep is key to feeling good and positive. Find out what works for you and get in that routine for maximum results.

For me, I like to read for about 15 to 20 minutes, then pray a little before I go to sleep. Whatever it is, you need to find it to change how you rest.

Energizing your body is so simple, but it means so much. We are not talking about a full-scale workout for 30 to 60 minutes. We are talking about three to five minutes of warming up, basically. Stretching your body, doing a little yoga, five pushups, five jumping jacks, five arm curls, or three minutes of jump rope—whatever works for you. All you want to do is get your blood flowing. By doing this, you are aiding your mind.

Our body and mind work in conjunction with each other. If one is out of whack, the other doesn't function like it should. If your back hurts, it's hard to concentrate—the same goes for your mind. If you get distracted, your body goes into automatic mode, and sometimes, it doesn't see things that are in the way, like walls, desks, someone else, stairs. Balance is required.

Meditation and prayer are easy tasks to accomplish. Research says, when we first wake up, our mind is blank. Just for that moment. The subconscious isn't working out any problems. Then, we think: What time is it? I need to get dressed. I have to be at work early today. What was I dreaming? This sets the mind to working, solving problems non-stop. So, before the mind gets too full from the day, meditate or pray.

We are talking about balance. If our spiritual self isn't at peace, we don't have complete balance, and without balance, it's hard to hold that positive energy consistently.

So, what are we talking about? We are talking about spending some time to clear or clarify your thoughts—putting everything in its proper perspective and releasing any negative thoughts to make room for the positive.

For those who prefer meditation, it means you want to go to a happy or peaceful place, more or less. You close your eyes, be still, and let your mind go. Along the journey to that place, several thoughts are going to come up, and you will address them, as needed, until you feel at peace. I know I make this sound simple—and it is—but you may need to practice a few times to get there. In five minutes, you can clear your mind for the day.

Praying is a little different, and each religion may do it differently. But all prayer goes for the same results of feeling at peace. When people pray, they are taking those thoughts and giving them to their god to get their help in resolving any issues, and in doing this, it puts the person's mind at peace. This works best for me.

This is for you spirit, your essence, or—some might say— your inner-self. We are not just physical beings: there's "that life" that's even hard for the professionals to explain. Nevertheless, it's part of us that needs to be recognized and considered in all we do.

Getting good rest, energizing the body, meditating every day, and doing these things along with making your bed, getting ready and dressed, and smiling at yourself in the morning, ensures you will have your positive energy flowing and ready for your day. Others will feed off your positivity, which will create a better environment for all.

I know most of you probably do some of these things—or maybe all of these things—without thinking about it. This is why I call this "Thought Talk". You need to think about actions in a positive way. Yeah, you do these things, but how have they affected you? Think about your feelings, and it makes everything more positive.

I want you to think about these two quotes every morning:

Daniel Gomez says, "The way you start your morning is the way your day is going to go."

Alec Stern says, "Invest in yourself the first thing in the morning."

Start your day with positive things! Be the Force of Positivity. Go ahead, give it a try.

CHAPTER 3

"WHAT WE SAY"

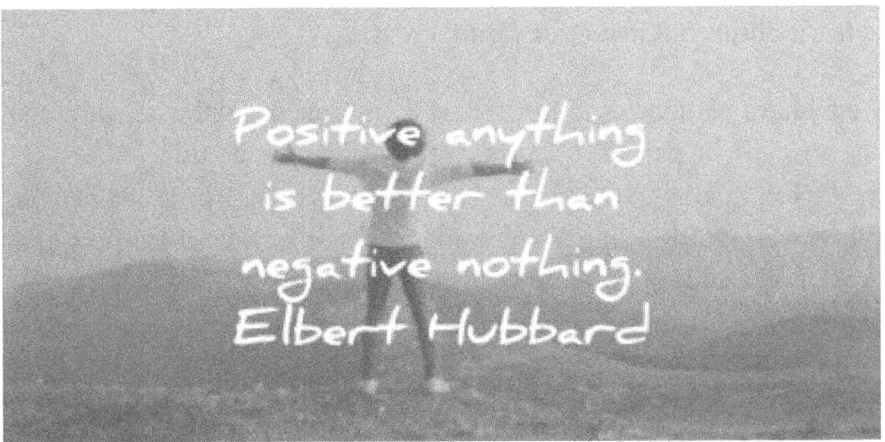

What we say says a lot about us and our mood. I'm not talking about "how we say it"—we'll get into that a little later. This chapter is about how many negative things we say all the time. We do it without thinking—to our kids, spouses, co-workers, etc. We do it while just replying to someone's comment or idea or just in general conversations.

This is because we just respond, and we don't really think. We don't respond to their mind or spirit, but to their physical self. For example: You arrive at work, and one of your co-workers starts walking to the door at the same time you do. You smile (a positive!) and ask, "How was your weekend?"

They say, "I had a good weekend. I finally got to clean and wax my car."

You respond, "Well, it's about time, but good for you."

Not a bad response, but how does their subconscious receive it? It's a negative; it picked up on the first part of the comment and killed any positive wave it might have started. I know the first part was just a tease, but it was still negative. Thinking before you speak is easy. You could have said, "Good for you. I'm glad you finally got it done." You still got to tease a little, but in a more positive way.

We all have tendencies to just talk with automatic responses, with you just trying to be part of the conversation. When we do this, I like to say we are just talking to the physical being. That's only a third of a person. When we talk, it is important we are talking to the whole person—mind, body, and spirit.

This is where "Thought Talk" comes from. A two-second conversation with your subconscious can make a lot of difference in the words you say, which can make a world of a difference in how you make someone else feel. Are you feeding them positive waves or negative energy?

Now, don't get me wrong. There are times when playful comments are fine, and we all know laughter is positive medicine. You will learn when the time is right for those, and when it's not. Just taking that two seconds for your subconscious to resolve what's best will also teach you when a little horsing-around is fine. The subconscious is where our mood starts—that why it's important to feed it positive things. If we don't, your emotions become negative and can be hard to resolve. In many cases, we let our spirit take over, and that's not always a good thing, because the spirit can be sad, mad, hurt, happy, etc. The spirit will then control the body's reaction to match that feeling.

Many times, we don't wait those two seconds, and we immediately start to react. We say things we don't mean, do things we regret, and hurt someone in the process. We, our person, only functions at its best when we are using the mind, body, and spirit together. Staying positive, acting positive, and being fed positivity from others is the only way to stay balanced.

Our subconscious takes in all the information we see, feel, hear, and read. It separates it, processes it, and communicates to you what the best outcomes are. This only takes a fraction of a second, so wait for it.

Also, this is where our endorphins live. They are what causes positive energy. When we stimulate our endorphins in a positive way—either by what we take in, or by what we send out— it creates a wave of positive emotions. Then, they work together with the body and spirit to react in a positive way.

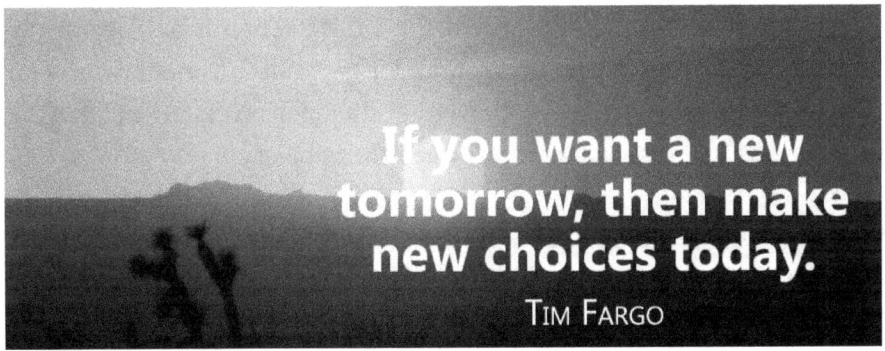

There was a study done by Stanford University in 1998 that showed how the usage of certain words can create either a positive or negative reaction in your subconscious. This reaction can affect how a person responds to you, or how they feel about you. The study found that certain reactions are common and could be beneficial for you to know about when you communicate.

This study took 240 subjects and tested them in several situations, which involved different scenarios, like instructional dialogues, group discussions, and stressful debates. During these studies, they evaluated how the brain reacted, and how the subject felt after tests.

During the tests that were instructional-related, they called subjects in, gave them instructions with the minimum amount of facts, and thanked them. They then sent them away to do the task.

In the second round, they did the same thing, but this time, they said the subject's name three times during the instruction.

The third round was the same as the second, but this time, the instructor told the subject that they thought that with their abilities, this would be a good assignment for them. The instructor noted their confidence in the subjects' abilities to do the assignment.

During these tests, they monitored the subjects' brains activity in the frontopolar cortex, medial temporal lobes, and the medial parietal cortex—the area where they believe the subconscious is. Also, after the instructions, the instructors questioned the subjects.

Brain activity grew from the first test to the second test, and it grew even more during the third test. The tests showed the subjects were more engaged in the third test, and they found the pattern was for the subjects to be more positive during the second and third tests.

From the questions on the first test, the subjects felt like they had to do the assignment because they were instructed to do so. They also didn't know if the instructor liked them or not, and they weren't 100-percent sure they could do the assignment. They also felt that their assignment was probably harder than the assignment given to the others. They didn't know that the assignments were the same for all subjects.

Things improved on the second test—when they mentioned the subject name at least three times. The subjects thought the instructor was nice and seemed to like them, so they were excited to attempt the assignment.

The third test—when they mentioned the subject's abilities and told them they could handle the assignments—the subjects felt like the instructor liked them, and he had trusted them to do them assignment. They were also sure they would complete the assignment.

This was just one of many tests they did. It's amazing how just a couple of words can make all the difference in attitudes and emotions. All we need to do is use positive reinforcement in the way we communicate.

I showed you this research for two reasons:

First, it was to show you how the subconscious mind works with what someone says to you. The more positive someone is towards you, the more positive waves you have in your mind. If you have prepared yourself from the start of your day, take the two seconds to listen to your subconscious. You will be the one saying the positive things, creating the waves, and getting positive things said back to you. Second, it was to show you what someone says, also has effect on what you say. The first trial, with just the given instructions, the participants didn't have anything positive to say. But, during the third trial, the instructors were saying positive thing to the participants, and in return, the participants had positive feedback. It's really THAT SIMPLE.

How many times have we said to someone, "Hey, I need to talk to you" or "I need to have a conversation with you?" This is talking to the physical person. It's a negative statement. You left the person feeling like they may have done something wrong they don't know about. What if you would have said, "Hey, you got a minute? If you don't mind, I need your help."

If you need answers, you may just need to say you need some clarification. Say, "I would like to talk to you about [whatever the subject is]."

Yes, this probably takes about three seconds longer to say, but it's worth it. You asked for permission. You showed respect You were courteous. What they had to say was important, and you asked for their help. All this is positive. Even if you are broaching something that is negative—like if they did something wrong, or if they gave bad advice—it is still better to start on a positive note. This could make the conversation go much more smoothly, and end with a better outcome.

Re-train yourself to wait the two seconds before you speak, and always say as many positive things as you can—it will build positivity around you, and will create a happy environment for everyone involved.

"Be the positive impact on the lives of others." — Roy T. Bennett

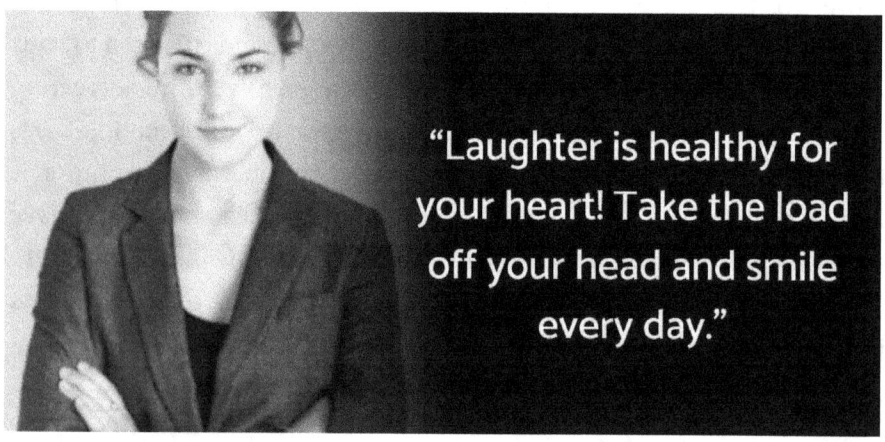

CHAPTER 4

HOW WE SAY IT

How we say things involves the words we use. Certain words or phrases in conversation can be positive, be encouraging, build confidence, build trust, and form a bond. This is important for everyone—parents, teachers, business people, friends, etc. This is even important if you are deal with an adversary. Knowing what words to use helps keep that positive wave growing.

I go back to a conversation with one of my mentors and preachers, John Fuller. He tells a story of three men sitting on a park bench. The first gentlemen says, "It's a good day."

Then, the second man says, "No, it's a great day."

Then the third man says, "No, it is a wonderful day." The three men look at each other and start to laugh. Then, one of them says, "I'm glad we agree."

The point of this conversation is that each man had his on perspective of the day. They were all correct, but how they described it was different. All three said positive things about the day—"wonderful", "great", "good"— and they all had the same, positive effect.

So, what I'm giving you are just some of the ways to communicate positively. You may find some positive words or phrases that work for you.

Let's get started:

Someone's name: When you are introduced to someone, you should always say their name back to them in your greeting, out of respect. It subconsciously makes them feel more confident. But did you know, if you continue to use their name several times during the conversation, you trigger their subconscious to think you like and trust them? You are continuing to build their confidence, and they are more apt to want to do something for you or with you.

This also helps you, even after you know someone well. Using their name in conversation triggers their subconscious the same way. This is an easy way to get the positive energy flowing in them. Once their positive energy wave starts flowing, it will help to keep your positive wave going.

Research says you should use their name at least three times during a conversation for it to make an impact. Most people like their name, so it might be helpful to tell them you like their name.

Not only is this a positive action, but if it's someone new to you, repeating their name will help you remember who they are. Remembering people's name is a positive note for you and will definitely make you feel better.

Permission: Asking someone their permission to join a conversation seems a little odd, but it's not. Everyone prefers to have a choice. So, it's good to ask if it is alright to ask them a question, or if they mind having a conversation, etc. When you do this, it tells their subconscious they are important and you trust them. All this is positive.

You can ask permission in several different ways. As I said above, you can ask to have a conversation or ask a question. You can also ask for their opinion or their recommendation. The one I use the most is probably, "Say, John, do you have a moment?" This not only gives them a choice, but it also gets their attention and their permission.

If you are in a sales or a leadership role, you understand this also forms a commitment with that person, because you use their name several times and asked for their permission. You caused positive waves in their subconscious, and it tells them you have built trust with them, you like them, they are important to you, and it makes them feel confident. All this is a positive influence, and this is only two things to help have a positive communication.

If you are in a leadership role or in sales, influencing someone is a good thing. You are trying to get someone to do what you want because they want to. Building one's confidence, trust, respect, and value is a good start.

This type of influence is also good in general conversation. You create a positive atmosphere for you and them. It doesn't matter if it is a friend, family member, or someone new—you want the conversation to be productive. Having a positive effect helps keep it that way.

"Positive thinking will let you do everything better than negative thinking will." — **Zig Ziglar**

"The achievement of a happy life is not only positively good for us, it is constructively good for those around us."

— **Lisa Cypers Kamen**

Little Favor: These are two powerful words. When you ask someone for a little favor, you have to use their name and ask for permission. In the subconscious, this is reinforcing they are important, you trust them, you like them, and you have confidence in them. All of this makes them want to help you, and you have their attention. This is all positive.

A joint research team from Harvard, New York University, and University of California worked with 1,000 participants and found that all participants had genetic traits that correlated to being supportive, submissive, helpful, and accepting—which means it is a natural, inherent behavior to want to help someone.

Asking for a little favor triggers this in their subconscious. You are asking them to do something they already subconsciously want to do. This would be a natural positive. But, this is also something you don't want to do all the time to a person, because at some point, it will make the other party feel like you are taking advantage of them, and that becomes a negative energy.

It is also important that I caution you to not use the term "big favor". Adding the "big" is negative, not positive. It means you are going to ask for a lot, which tells their subconscious they may not be able to do all you ask, before you ever ask the favor. It would be better to just ask for a favor. You will still get the same, positive response as asking for a little favor, but adding "little" makes it sound easy.

Small talk: In today's world, where everyone is on the go, we forget about the small talk. This is where we take the time to share some details about ourselves and let others share a little detail about themselves. This can be great, or small. If you are talking to someone you know, it can be about what you were doing earlier, or what you plan to do later.

If it's someone new, talking a little about your family might be good. It can lead them into talking about their family. Maybe talk about your hobbies or activities or tell a story. All we are trying to do is not only learn a little about them, but to also make them more comfortable. This also makes you more human and personable.

This is something to remember: the more we know about a person, the better we know how to communicate with them in a positive manner. If I know someone had had a bitter divorce, I know not to ask or make comments related to marriage or spouses. Communicating positively has a lot to do with who the person is within the conversation.

Small talk tells a lot about someone. Some of this has to do with telltale signs we will get into a little later in the book, but you can tell what excites them, subjects they may be interested in, and even if they are naturally a positive person or not. All you need to do is just listen and pay attention to the changes in their voice.

Most of this is simple. The problem is, you haven't really stopped and thought about what, why, and how someone says something. The time is now. It can only make a better communicator out of you.

Accessibility: If you are a manager or leader, you are still part of your team. Making yourself accessible not only shows others you are still part of the team, but also that you are available for questions and help. They will make more of an effort in keeping you informed. This can be as easy as keeping your door open, walking around the work area, and speaking to your team daily.

This is always good for your family and friends. They need to feel you are accessible for conversations and advice—or that you are just someone who will listen to them about their day. When someone thinks about calling you with good or bad news, it's a positive thing. Making them feel you are there for them is not only comforts them, but also builds a bond of trust. These are positive actions—building trust, being comforted, and being there for them any time—all of this is positive.

Facts: You can use all the positive words and phrases to keep a conversation positive. You can even add a little small talk to make everyone comfortable. However, if you don't know all the facts on the subject of conversation, it could very easily head to the negative side.

If you are going to have a conversation with someone on something that's been said, gather as much information as you can before you have the conversation. If you are not sure of the information, your conversation may need to be a question and answer session. Approach it in the same way you would if you were needing clarification on something. Always form your question as if you are asking for their knowledge. That keeps it positive.

If you are talking about something that is more technical, take the time to become as knowledgeable as possible. By doing so, it not only shows confidence, but it also makes the other party feel more relaxed, make them have a more open discussions with you–which is positive.

I know most of you know other positive words that can be used, but I will list just a few of them you can use in a conversation:

1. Good job!
2. That's great!
3. Looks good!
4. You are very knowledgeable.
5. I love this!

6. You convince me.
7. I need your advice.
8. I need your opinion.
9. You're a natural.
10. With your ability…
11. Can you help me?

CHAPTER 5

WHAT NOT TO SAY

Here are some things you should never do or try during a conversation. What we are trying to do here is avoid any reason for the conversation to turn negative. Again, these are some things I suggest; you may find others that with be just as useful.

Never ask for big favors. The "big" throws out a negative energy. They will automatically wonder if they can do the favor before you even tell them what it is. Asking for a little favor is positive, and subconsciously makes them feel you like and trust them. Funny how one word can make such a difference.

To want something big is a large request, in itself—no wonder it's a negative. Even if you are needing a big favor for some reason, break it down into timely, small favors. This way, you should get the results you want, while keeping things positive.

Never demand anything. Demanding makes the person feel you don't like them, and they will subconsciously resent you for it. In some businesses, the pressure to complete an assignment is great, but don't let yourself reach a point where you think you have to demand results to get the job done. If you reach this point, it means you failed somewhere down the road. This negative impact will make your team less productive, and you might lose employees.

If you should demand something from a friend or family member, they will automatically sense a negativity from you, and you will cause harm to your relationship. The last thing you want is to cause any negative thoughts. Keep the "big" out of it and stay on the positive side of the conversation.

Never dismiss the other party's solutions, answers, or opinion— unless you have all the facts. If you do, and the facts show their answer was reasonable, they will subconsciously feel you degraded them, and they will lose some respect for you. They will also think their opinion doesn't matter to you. Apologizing will help, but it may not heal the wound. Then, all your positive work goes down the drain.

If you must have a discussion about an issue, try to have all the facts. Once the facts are on the table, the discussion can be more positive. If the facts don't support the other party's solutions, answers, or opinions, then it is easy to explain why you dismiss them. It can be done in an encouraging way—like, "Your opinion would be a good one, but the facts say this", or "I like the way you think, and your solution is so close, but as you can see, that wouldn't work."

Never be too proud to acknowledge when you are wrong. To acknowledge this makes you human, just like them. They will subconsciously like you more. Admitting you were wrong also shows you are honest and will be responsible for your actions—you don't blame others for your mistakes.

We all make mistakes. The sooner you acknowledge it, the better. If you put this off, you are only creating more problems. The other party is expecting you to say something about the mistake, so the longer you wait, the less they trust you and the more they doubt your decisions.

Own it. Be humble and explain you will try not to make the mistake again. Thank them for understanding and being on your side. This will build a tighter bond and keep your relationship positive.

Never think you can't be part of a problem. Sometimes, people forget they are part of a vested relationship— they think of themselves as outside of the problem—but in reality, they are the problem. Sometimes, we need to allow ourselves the two seconds to process the problem before we confront the other parties, or we may need to get more informed. We should always be evaluating our thoughts, words, and actions, and we should accept the fact that we can be the problem and learn how to deal with it to make us better and more positive.

Just like acknowledging a mistake, you need to acknowledge when you are the reason for a problem. Reaching out to your team or friends for help in resolving the issue you created will keep the trust and bond you have with them. This is a positive action that everyone involved will benefit from.

Never let your emotions take over. Sometimes, this is easier said than done, but if you do let your emotions take over, you lost control as a person, a friend, a leader, or a mentor. It's not that we don't have emotions—we are going to get upset or mad from time to time. It's how we handle these emotions that matters. Others can see the emotion, so when we act, we must act with our good judgment and in a civil manner.

If we lose control of our emotions, and fly off the handle, we cause more damage than good. Also, if we can't control our emotions, others will wonder what else we can't control. Always be the person in control. If you are angry, step back and take two seconds to think before you speak. This can be one of the most crucial times during a conversation. It will be up to you to keep everything on the positive side. I never said it would always be easy. You are the one with the tools to keep everything on a positive note. Never assume the other party does.

There is nothing wrong with being upset, sad, or angry. It is natural. As a leader, keeping your composure and staying civil is a must. Good leaders never let something control how they conduct themselves. Staying calm may be the one thing that keeps things moving in a positive way.

> *"Take time to feed your soul, compliment yourself, pamper yourself, smile at yourself, think positive thoughts, and speak life. Watch how you talk to yourself – because you are listening."*
> — ***Germany Kent***

CHAPTER 6

FAMILY AND FRIENDS

Family and friends are some of the easiest and hardest people to talk to. In reality, we communicate differently to family and friends than we do co-workers, strangers, acquaintances, and even boyfriends and girlfriends. In most cases, we are more open and honest with each other. Also, each party is more forgiving when one's feelings are hurt.

Remember, you are the Force of Positivity, and communicating with your family and friends will probably challenge this from time to time. You need to be the one who controls the atmosphere and attitudes.

There are many things families and friends can do to become more effective communicators, and in turn, can improve the quality of their relationships. Families and friends can improve their communication skills by following some suggestions for building effective family communication.

Communicate frequently: One of the most difficult challenges facing families today is finding time to spend together. According to a recent *Wall Street Journal* survey, 40-percent of the respondents stated that lack of time was a greater problem for them than lack of money.

With our busy schedules, it is difficult to find sufficient time to spend with one another in meaningful conversation. It is extremely important for families and friends to make time to communicate: talk in the car; turn the TV off and eat dinner together; schedule informal, or formal, family meetings to talk about important issues that affect your family. The same thing applies to your friends and your children. There are many creative ways to make time to communicate with others.

Communicate clearly and directly: Healthy families and friends communicate their thoughts and feelings in a clear and direct manner. This is especially important when attempting to resolve problems that arise between family or friends. Indirect and vague communication will not only fail to resolve problems, but it will also contribute to a lack of intimacy and emotional bonding between all.

Be an active listener: an essential aspect of effective communication is listening to what others are saying. Being an active listener involves you trying your best to understand the other person's point of view. Whether you are listening to a spouse, a child, or a friend, it is important to pay close attention to their verbal and non-verbal messages. As an active listener, you must acknowledge and respect the other person's perspective. For example, when listening, you should nod your head or say, "I understand", which conveys to the other person that you care about what they have to say. It's positive. Another aspect of active listening is seeking clarification if you do not understand what the other person said. This can be done by simply asking, "What did you mean when you said this?" or "Did I understand you correctly?" Active listening involves acknowledging and respecting the other person's point of view.

In order for effective communication to take place within relationships between families and friends, individuals must be open and honest with one another. This openness and honesty will set the stage for trusting relationships. Without trust, families and friends cannot build strong relationships with you. Parents, especially, are responsible for providing a safe environment that allows family members to openly express their thoughts and feelings.

Think about the person with whom you are communicating: Not all people communicate in the same manner, nor on the same level. This is especially true of young children. When communicating with young children, it is important for adults to listen carefully to what the children are saying without making unwarranted assumptions. It is also important to take into consideration the ages and maturity levels of children. Parents cannot communicate with children the same way they communicate with their spouse, because the child may not be old enough to understand.

Pay attention to non-verbal messages: In addition to carefully listening to what is being said, effective communicators also pay close attention to the non-verbal behaviors of other family members. For example: a spouse, child, or a friend may say something verbally, but their facial expressions or body language may be telling you something completely different. In cases such as these, it is important to find out how the person is really feeling.

Be Positive: While it is often necessary to address problems and negative situations between family and friends, effective communication is primarily positive. Marital and family researchers have discovered that unhappy relationships are often the result of negative communication patterns (e.g., criticism, contempt, defensiveness). In fact, John Gottman and his colleagues have found that satisfied married couples had five positive interactions to every one negative interaction. Couples who are very dissatisfied with their relationships typically engage in more negative interactions than positive. It is very important for family and friends to verbally compliment and encourage one another.

When communicating with your children, it can be challenging because of the levels of maturity. Remember these tips when dealing with your children:

Be available: Make time in everyone's busy schedule to stop and talk about things. Even ten minutes a day without distractions for you and your child to talk can make a big difference in forming good communication habits. Turn off the television or radio. Give your undivided attention to your child. Sit down and look at your child while you talk. Those few minutes a day can be of great value.

Be a good listener: When you listen to your child, you help your child feel loved and valued. Ask your child about his feelings on a subject. If you are not clear about what your child is saying, repeat what you are hearing to be sure that you understand what your child is trying to say. You do not have to agree with what your child is saying to be a good listener. Sharing his thoughts with you helps your child calm down, so later he can listen to you.

Show empathy: This means tuning in to your child's feelings and letting him know you understand. If your child is sad or upset, a gentle touch or hug may let him know that you understand those sad or bad feelings. Do not tell your child what he thinks or feels. Let him express those feelings. Be sure not to minimize these feelings by saying things like, "It's silly to feel that way" or "You'll understand when you get older." His feelings are real to him and should be respected.**Be a good role model**:

Remember, children learn by example. Use words and tones in your voice you want your child to use. Make sure that your tone of voice and what you do send the same message. For example, if you laugh when you say, "No, don't do that," the message will be confusing. Be clear in your directions. Once you get the message across, do not wear out your point. If you use words to describe your feelings, it will help your child to learn to do the same. When parents use feeling words, such as, "It makes me feel sad when you won't do what I ask you to do," instead of screaming or name calling, children learn to do the same. The same goes when you are happy about what your child has done. Show this emotion for the positive affect.

*"Listen with curiosity. Speak with honesty. Act with integrity. The greatest problem with communication is we don't listen to understand. We listen to reply. When we listen with curiosity, we don't listen with the intent to reply. We listen for what's behind the words." — **Roy T. Bennett***

CHAPTER 7

COMMUNICATION SKILLS

COMMUNICATIONS

Communication skills are abilities you use when giving and receiving different kinds of information. Some examples include communicating ideas, feelings, or events happening around you. Communication skills involve listening, speaking, observing, and empathizing. It is also helpful to understand the differences in how to communicate through face-to-face interactions, phone conversations, and digital communications—like email and social media.

There are different types of communication skills you can learn and practice to help you become an effective communicator. Many of these skills work together, making it important to practice communication skills in different contexts whenever possible. Your audience, or followers, can affect your type of communication. You can still keep the positive approach as you develop these skills, **though.**

Active listening: This means paying close attention to the person who is speaking to you. People who are active listeners are well-regarded by their coworkers because of the attention and respect they offer. While it seems simple, this is a skill that can be hard to develop and improve. You can be an active listener by focusing on the speaker, avoiding distractions— like cell phones, laptops, or other projects— and by preparing questions, comments, or ideas to thoughtfully respond with.

Adapting your communication style to your audience: Different styles of communication are appropriate in different situations. To make the best use of your communication skills, it's important to consider your audience and the most effective format to communicate with them.

For example, if you are communicating with a potential employer, it's better to send a formal email or call them on the phone. Depending on the situation, you may even need to send a formal, typed letter over other forms of communication. In the workplace, you may find it's easier to communicate complex information in person, or via video conference, rather than in a long, dense email.

Friendliness: In friendships, characteristics such as honesty and kindness often foster trust, understanding, and positivity. The same characteristics are important in workplace relationships. When you're working with others, approach your interactions with a positive attitude, keep an open mind, and ask questions to help you understand where they're coming from. Small gestures—such as asking someone how they're doing, smiling as they speak, or offering praise for work well done—can help you foster productive relationships with both colleagues and managers.

Confidence: In the workplace, people are more likely to respond to ideas that are presented with confidence. There are many ways to appear confident, including by making eye contact when you're addressing someone, sitting up straight with your shoulders open, and preparing ahead of time, so your thoughts are polished. You'll find confident communication comes in handy, not just on the job, but during the job interview process as well.

Giving and receiving feedback: Strong communicators are able to accept critical feedback and provide constructive input. This should be in a positive way—feedback should answer questions, provide solutions, or help strengthen the project or topic at hand.

Volume and clarity: When you're speaking, it's important to be clear and audible. Adjusting your speaking voice so you can be heard in a variety of settings is a skill, and it's critical to communicating effectively. Speaking too loudly may by disrespectful or awkward in certain settings. If you're unsure, read the room to see how others are communicating.

Empathy: Having empathy means you can understand and share the emotions of others. This communication skill is important in both team and one-on-one settings. In both cases, you will need to understand other people's emotions and select an appropriate response. For example, if someone is expressing anger or frustration, empathy can help you acknowledge and diffuse their emotion. At the same time, being able to understand when someone is feeling positive and enthusiastic can help you get support for your ideas and projects.

Respect: A key aspect of respect is knowing when to initiate communication and when to respond. In a team or group setting, allowing others to speak without interruption is seen as a necessary communication skill that is tied to respectfulness. Respectfully communicating also means using your time with someone else wisely—staying on topic, asking clear questions, and responding fully to any questions you've been asked. These are positive steps.

Understanding nonverbal cues: A great deal of communication happens through nonverbal cues, such as body language, facial expressions, and eye contact. When you're listening to someone, you should be paying attention to what they're saying, as well as their nonverbal language. By the same measure, you should be conscious of your own body language when you're communicating, to ensure you're sending appropriate cues to others.

Responsiveness: Whether you're returning a phone call, or sending a reply to an email, fast communicators are viewed as more effective than those who are slow to respond. One method is to consider how long your response will take: is this a request or question you can answer in the next five minutes? If so, it may be a good idea to address it as soon as you see it. If it's a more complex request or question, you can still acknowledge that you've received the message, then let the other person know you will respond in full later.

With experience and practice, you can learn and improve on communication skills. Start by identifying your strengths, and then, practice and develop those areas. Here are some tips on how to improve:

Ask a close friend or colleague for constructive criticism: It can be hard to know how you are perceived as a communicator. To get an objective opinion, ask a trusted friend for their honest feedback. Understanding your areas of improvement for communication can help you identify what to focus on.

Practice improving communication habits: Many communication skills are habits you have developed over time. You can improve those skills by practicing new habits that make you a better communicator. That might include being more responsive to communications when they are sent, reminding yourself to maintain eye contact, practicing giving positive feedback, and asking questions in conversations.

Attend communication skills workshops or classes: There are several online and offline seminars, workshops, and classes that can help you be a better communicator. These classes may include instructions, roleplaying, written assignments, and open discussions.

Seek opportunities to communicate: Seek out opportunities both on and off the job that requires you to use communication skills. This will help you keep good skills fresh, while also allowing you the opportunity to practice new skills.

While there are several communication skills you will use in different scenarios, there are a few ways you can be effective and a positive communicator at work:

Be clear and concise: Making your message as easy to consume as possible reduces the chance of misunderstandings, speeds up projects, and helps others quickly understand your goals. Instead of speaking in long, detailed sentences, practice reducing your message down to its core meaning. While providing context is helpful, it is best to give the most necessary information when trying to communicate your idea, instruction, or message in a positive way.

Practice empathy: Understanding your colleagues' feelings, ideas, and goals can help you when communicating with them. For example, you might need help from other departments to get a project started. If they are not willing to help, or if they have concerns, practicing empathy can help you position your message in a way that addresses their apprehension.

Assert yourself: At times, it is necessary to be assertive to reach your goals— whether you are asking for a raise, seeking project opportunities, or resisting an idea you don't think will be beneficial. While presenting with confidence is an important part of the workplace, you should always be respectful in conversation. Keeping an even tone, and providing sound reasons for your assertions, will help others be receptive to your thoughts.

Be calm and consistent: When there is a disagreement or conflict, it can be easy to bring emotion into your communications. It is important to remain calm when communicating with others in the workplace. Be aware of your body language by not crossing your arms or rolling your eyes. Maintaining consistent body language and keeping an even tone of voice can help you reach a positive conclusion peacefully and productively.

Use and read body language: Body language is a key part of communications in the workplace. Pay close attention to the messages people are sending with their facial expressions and movements. You should also pay close attention to the way you might be communicating with your own body language.

Parts of this are from research done by the University of Missouri on "Social Communication"

CHAPTER 8

BODY LANGUAGE

We spend our lives learning how to decode other people's nonverbal cues. While we're busy trying to decode their messages, they are also trying to decode ours. There are times when you want other people to know exactly how you're feeling, especially when those feelings are both positive and reciprocated. This isn't always easy to do, particularly if you're not a very emotional type of person. At other times, however, you definitely want to hide your inner feelings. To avoid emotional leakage, you may have to work doubly hard. Depending on the situation, you may need to put on your Lady Gaga-style poker face.

Body language is just that—the language of the body. You may think that you only show your emotions through your face, but that is only the tip of the iceberg. Your entire body participates in the business of either showing or hiding your mental state.

To control that display, means you have to control your body's cues. This guide will show you how, starting from the top down. By the time you're done, you'll have a greater understanding of how even the most seemingly insignificant bodily gestures can provide key signals of your emotions.

Your Head: Starting at the very top of your head is, of course, your scalp. Your hair can actually tell a great deal about your emotional state. People have bad hair days for many reasons—it might be your mood as much as it is the weather. When you're stressed, for example, you may forget to run a comb through your frazzled locks. At a glance, people will know you're not feeling completely pulled together. Similarly, a bed head after a long night out may be sexy to some, but it's not the look you want to cultivate to impress at the office or your kid's PTA meeting. Cut, color, or amount of hair aside— the fact that it's groomed lets others know that you're in control of the way your day is developing. If you don't have any hair, the problem is solved, but with your forehead more in evidence, you'll be giving away other nonverbal cues when you're frowning.

There's not much you can do to change the way your permanent facial features communicate your feelings—your nose just is what it is. However, the parts of your face that reflect what psychologists call "**display rules**" play a vital role in letting others know exactly how you're feeling and maybe even exactly what you're thinking. The most important of these are the tiniest movements involving the muscles around your eyes and mouth, called "**micro-expressions**". One reason they are so important to understanding body language is they can completely contradict the impression you're trying to create by what you're saying. You may want to hide your feelings of fear that you have when talking to someone you want to impress, but the little pulling back of the muscles around your mouth instead shows that you're panicking on the inside. If you make a grimace now, you'll know what I mean.

While you're grimacing, pay attention to what's happening to your forehead—bald people, take note! You're probably raising your eyebrows, another cue to the discomfort you're feeling. People don't just show micro-expressions of fear when they're afraid; they also do so when they're lying. So, if you're trying to hide a little white lie, make sure you control those little facial muscles, too. I'm not advising that you *do* lie, just telling you that if you've got no other choice, you'll have to stop that mini grimace from appearing. Convince yourself that you truly like your best friend's new hairdo, even if you think it's hideous, and your compliment will seem sincere.

Your eyes also communicate many important cues about your inner state. Most importantly, you need to strike the right balance between too much and too little staring at who you're speaking to. Too much, and you can make the other person uncomfortable. Too little, and you'll seem disinterested. You also want to avoid making superfluous, insulting gestures—such as the sarcastic eye roll—even if you think you won't be detected.

On the positive side, there's nothing quite like a friendly twinkle in the eyes to put other people at ease and take an immediate **liking** to you. Again, this doesn't need to be over the top, nor should the eye twinkle be brought out at solemn occasions. Under ordinary circumstances, however, a twinkle can break the ice, make you appear to be a welcoming person, and give others a cue to the fascinating wit that lurks within you. Be careful, though, that you don't go so far as to wink.

It's getting time to move on to the rest of the body, but before I do, I need to mention the chin and neck. I've never completely understood how stubbornness could be interpreted from the shape of the chin, given that it's a fixed facial structure. However, if you habitually jut it out in front of you, it's possible people will assume that you're somewhat obstinate, so avoid doing that. Your neck, similarly, is a fixed, bodily feature, but the way you use it to hold up your head is very un-fixed. Use your neck to hold your head straight and help keep your eyes in front of you, rather than staring at the floor or ceiling—which are bad body language signals—and you'll look poised and self-confident.

Your torso: With your neck holding your head high, you'll be more likely to align your posture. Keep your back straight, and your shoulders from lurching forward, to add to the impression you're confident and in control of your feelings. On the other hand, if you want to appeal to someone's sympathetic side, you can sag a little all around, because you will look more in need of help. A chronic sagging posture, though, tells other people you don't feel very good about yourself. Keep yourself upright, but not ramrod-stiff, and you let the world know you feel comfortable in your body and feel good about yourself.

Attached to your upper torso are, of course, your arms and hands. These upper limbs provide many opportunities for body language failures if you're not careful. You communicate anxiety or boredom when your hands fidget, and anger, when you cross your arms tightly. If you place your arms akimbo, you can unintentionally look arrogant. Of course, if you want to look angry or arrogant, these are great ways to communicate those feelings. If you'd rather not, then find some neutral way to keep your hands and arms from getting in the way of the positive impression you want to make. I was once told, by a very accomplished colleague, that the best thing to do with your hands while you're sitting, is to gently hold them together in your lap. The folded hands keep you from over-gesticulating—another body language trap that can cause your feelings to spill out by the gallon. When you're standing, you need to find a similarly neutral way of letting your hands rest comfortably, either at your sides, or on some other convenient resting place.

Your legs: Now onto the lower limbs. When you're in full view of someone else, whether sitting or standing, you're giving away a wide array of important cues with your legs. Tightly crossing them while you're sitting in a chair presents a "closed" view of yourself to others, as if you're trying to build a mini fortress around yourself. Splaying them out carelessly in front of you sends just the opposite message. You want to seem open, relaxed, and comfortable, but not so much that you look sloppy and ready to fall asleep. Women wearing skirts have obvious reasons to pay attention to the way they hold their legs. In fact, if you happen to be wearing a skirt that's too short, you probably will feel a bit awkward and nervous about a wardrobe malfunction. That anxiety can spill over to the rest of your body language, causing the situation to rapidly deteriorate— as others will certainly notice your grave discomfort.

Anxiety can translate directly into unconscious leg-shaking or foot-tapping. People with jittery legs burn off more calories, but there are definitely better ways to work off those extra pounds—at least when you're in public situations. Shaking your legs while sitting sends a giant message to everyone around you feel anxious or irritable—or both. Your legs are the largest area of your body, so when they move, it's pretty hard for others not to notice. You can cure yourself of this **bad habit** by replacing the shaking motion with another action that will simultaneously calm you down. Crossing your legs at the ankles is the equivalent to folding your hands in your lap and doing both at the same time will greatly settle your feelings— while it also ramps up your poise factor.

Your feet: I said head-to-toe, and that's where we are going to end this tour of your body language cues. As I indicated above, shaking your legs communicates anxiety, and when you shake those legs, you inevitably shake those feet. However, your feet can get you into trouble with your body language all on their own. Tapping your toes is one way to show that you're in a hurry and anxious to get moving. You may want to tap your toes if you're trying to get someone's attention and don't want to say something rude. It's a little way of signaling that you're feeling time-pressured without yelling or engaging in sarcastic eye-rolling. However, you do so at a risk: you may be ignored or perceived as rude. Better to handle your feelings of annoyance over being made to wait by politely voicing your concerns.

Your feet also communicate confidence or fear by the way they move you from place to place. Your stride should be strong, and your gait as steady as you can manage, depending on your age and health. When you practice good posture, it will be easier to walk in a self-confident manner. On the other hand, slouching, slumping, or skulking makes you seem afraid of where you're heading. By doing so, it suggests you fear the direction you're taking. Wearing the right shoes can help cinch the deal. Flip-flops, four-inch stilettos, or shoes that just don't fit, can cause you to teeter, or worse— fall. It's **hard to recover your self-composure** after taking an embarrassing tumble.

To sum it all up, this guide should give you plenty to work on if you'd like to improve the image you project to others, especially employers you're **trying to impress** or potential partners you'd like to date. To seal the deal, take the ultimate, but most challenging step. Instead of using your phone just to catch videos of cute pet tricks to post on YouTube, turn it on you and record yourself doing ordinary, everyday activities. You'll be able to diagnose the characteristic bodily language cues that convey too much, too little, or just the wrong message about how you're feeling. Partner up with a friend or loved one and review the videos, looking for the cues that you most need to work on improving.

Part of the information above was developed by counseling psychologist, and former University of Massachusetts professor, **Alan Ivey.** He pioneered this method of micro-training to help counselors improve the way they communicate to their clients.

Your body's actions, consciously and unconsciously, reflect your mental state. Learning to control the cues you communicate to others will invariably boost not only the way you look, but the way you feel.

Here are some examples:

1. **Arms crossed across the chest:** Sitting or standing with your arms crossed across your chest is nearly always seen as defensive body language. When you do it, you're closed off and disengaged. You may appear angry or stubborn.

   If you see someone holding this position, remember that it could indicate the temperature where you are is too cold. It could also mean they're tired, or simply supporting their shoulders in an armless chair.

2. **Smile:** Smiles can mean different things, depending on the exact facial expression. There are happy smiles, shy smiles, warm smiles, and ironic smiles. The Duchenne smile consists of pulling up the corners of your mouth while squeezing your eyes to make crow's feet. It's considered a genuine smile, as opposed to a fake smile where you just expose your teeth.

   When you display an authentic Duchenne smile, you let people know you're approachable and friendly.

3. **Tapping your fingers:** When you tap your fingers, you appear impatient, and possibly, nervous about waiting.

4. **Tilting your head to one side:** When you tilt your head to the side, it usually means you're listening intently and are deeply interested in finding out the information you're being told. It can also mean you're concentrating very hard.

5. **Steepling your fingers:** Holding your fingertips together and your palms apart, lets people know you have authority and control. Bosses and politicians use this gesture often to show they're in charge.

6. **Crossing your legs:** The way you cross your legs can tell others a lot about you, and how you're feeling at any given moment. If you cross them at the ankle, it may show that you're trying to hide something. If you cross them at the knee, but point your knees away from the other person, you show you're uncomfortable with them. In most cases, the best option is to plant your feet firmly on the floor.

7. **Pulling your ear:** When you tug on your ear, it shows that you're trying to make a decision, but just haven't gotten there, yet. You

8. **Putting your head in your hands:** When you put your head in your hands, it might mean that you're bored, as if you're so weary of life you just can't hold your head up anymore. Or, it can mean you're upset, or so ashamed, you don't want to show your face.

9. **Standing up straight:** Standing erect with good posture shows you feel confident.

10. **Gesturing with your hands open and palms up:** What you do with your hands makes a big difference in whether people trust you or not. Hold your hands open, and gesture with your palms up to show that, no, you don't have anything hidden from them.

11. **Eye contact:** You need to make eye contact with the person you're talking to if you want them to feel comfortable with the conversation and accept what you have to say. **Scientists suggest** that most people are comfortable with eye contact of about 3.2

seconds at a time— if you're a stranger. When you become a friend, they don't usually mind having eye contact with you for longer at a time.

12. **Looking down:** Looking at the floor or ground makes you appear weak and unconfident. Unless there's something you need to discuss down there, you need to keep your eyes on the level of the other person's face. When you break eye contact, as you should every few seconds, try looking to the side.

13. **Rubbing your hands together:** Want to show how excited you are about a new project? Just rub your hands together vigorously.

14. **Twisting your hair:** Often, movies and TV shows use the gesture of twisting the hair to show flirting. That may be the meaning you get when someone twists their hair, especially if they look up at you through their lashes while they do it.

   However, if you're in a job interview, and you idly twist your hair, you'll only look like you're nervous and uncomfortable.

15. **Micro-expression**: Micro-expressions are extremely brief facial expressions that happen in about one-twenty-fifth of a second. They happen when you're trying to hold back your emotions. When you see someone showing a micro-expression, it usually means that they're trying to conceal something from you. However, if you learn to spot them, you can gain the advantage in any type of interaction.

16. **Walking briskly:** When you want to show your self-confidence, walk briskly and with purpose. Whether you're going somewhere specific or not, walk as if you're striding confidently toward an important destination.

17. **Placing your hand on your cheek:** When you touch your cheek with your hand, you show you're thinking and carefully evaluating the information you're receiving. When you see someone do this while you're talking to them, you can usually assume they're taking you seriously enough to consider what you're saying.

18. **Rubbing your eye:** When you rub your eye, it usually means you doubt, or disbelieve, what you're hearing. If you someone is rubbing their eye as you speak, you might benefit from stopping and asking for their feedback, so you can address their doubts.

19. **Rubbing or touching your nose:** When you rub or touch your nose, you appear dishonest. If you do it in a conversation that requires openness and honesty, you'll have trouble accomplishing your goals. And, if you see someone else rubbing their nose, it's a good indication you need to be careful not to automatically believe everything they tell you.

20. **Standing with your hands clasped behind your back:** Take a position with your hands clasped behind your back, and others may read this as anger, apprehension, or frustration. It may feel like a nice, casual pose, but in reality, it can make others uncomfortable and wary of you.

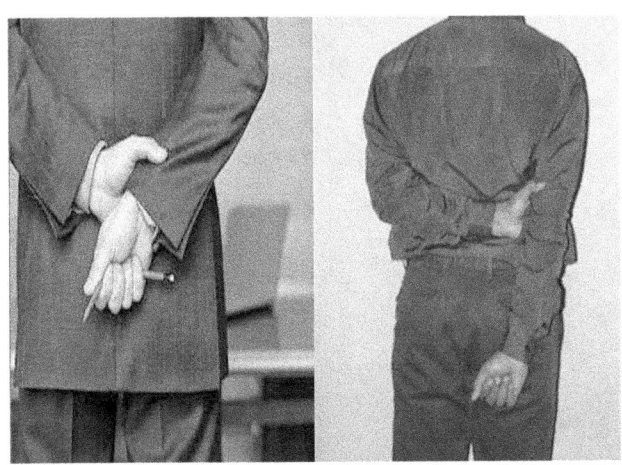

21. **Pinching the bridge of your nose:** When you close your eyes and pinch the bridge of your nose, you seem to be making a negative evaluation of what's happening in the conversation. If someone takes this pose with you, you may need to take a different approach in enlisting their support for your goal.

22. **Standing with your hands on your hips:** This pose is tricky. In some cases, it can mean you're feeling angry and may behave aggressively. In others, it may simply mean you're enthusiastic and ready to get something done.

CHAPTER 9

STORY SPEAK

So, what is "story speak"? It is a way to connect with your audience, whether it's a group of people, or an individual, by telling a story related to the subject. It's can be as short as a few words, but it must be told in color— per Nicholas Boothman, author of *The Irresistible Power of Story Speak*. "In color" means we must have audio, visual, and emotional elements to the story. Researchers say these are the three ways we all communicate.

I always felt a little uncomfortable telling personal stories and don't feel I'm very good at doing it, even today. But, I continue to work on it, because I also know the power it has.

Here are some of Mr. Boothman's own words on the subject, taken from one of the articles published about him.

> *"Research shows Story Speakers earn more, out-perform, do better in school and college, get hired and promoted faster, and get better service in-person and over the phone than fact-speakers."*

What is Story Speak? When Warren Buffett—the second-richest man in the U.S. and holder of the unofficial title, "America's Greatest Story Speaker"—was asked, "Do you enjoy your work?", he replied, "I tap-dance to work." That's Story Speak.

Martin Luther King, Jr.'s "I Have a Dream" speech was delivered in Story Speak, as was Steve Jobs's legendary Stanford-commencement speech in 2005. Queen Elizabeth I inspired her troops to victory with it in 1588 when she said, "I have the body of a woman; but the heart and stomach of a king."

Story Speak brings brands to life, strengthens marketing impacts, and forms the foundation of all growth strategies. The names PayPal, Apple, and Windows are all Story Speak. Mohammed Ali's saying, "float like a butterfly, sting like a bee", is Story Speak, too.

Almost every successful book, movie, or song ever written, relies on Story Speak to connect with emotions— as does every riveting conversation, presentation, and speech. In 1975, two screenwriters walked into a Hollywood producer's office and said three words: "Jaws in space." Then, the blockbuster movie *Alien* was born—pure Story Speak.

"Great communicators, since the beginning of time, have used Story Speak to change attitudes and behaviors, rally and inspire loyalty, and fire up the imagination." --**N. Boothman**

Ask any high school student who their favorite teacher is, and then, ask why. Chances are the answer will be, "because she makes things more interesting" or "because he tells stories". When educators Story Speak, they keep their students engaged and interested by transforming learning into lively experiences.

These teachers know that a great storyteller must first capture and hold the student's attention, and second, transport them into another world. And, they know the way to keep those students in that other world is by continually increasing the tension in the story until the conclusion is reached, the lesson is learned, and the message is delivered. This strategy doesn't just apply to motivating school children--it's everywhere in society. Advertisers polish their stories, social media spreads them, politicians bend them, religions exalt them, and motivational speakers use them to capture the hearts and minds of their audiences to transport them onto new horizons.

In business, when things get competitive, it's all about the story. Today's corporate leaders like stories, because they bring their company's heritage to life in the imagination. They share their stories with their customers, their staff, and their new hires. They live them. Corporate leaders Story Speak their visions and goals. Successful entrepreneurs Story Speak naturally. They use stories and word pictures to quickly get their ideas across in a tasty manner to make them stick. They talk about planting seeds, bearing fruit, and cutting out the deadwood. Sales-people know their stories are as—if not more—important as their products to build trust and reinforce their brand.

In healthcare, patients and doctors have long understood the power of telling and listening to personal accounts. Patients want to hear the stories of other patients who've gone through the same thing.

Researchers know the placebo effect is a perfect example of the power of the imagination to engage forces beyond a patient's conscious control— "Give them a pill. Tell them a story. Watch what happens."

The Annals of Internal Medicine recently published a study examining the effects of storytelling on high blood pressure. In the test group, listening to personal stories helped achieve and maintain a drop in blood pressure as effectively as adding more medication. "Telling and listening to stories is the way we make sense of our lives," said Dr. Thomas K. Houston, lead author of the study at the University of Massachusetts Medical School in Worcester. "That natural tendency has the potential to alter behavior and improve health."

Now here's my example of Story Speak:

Back in 2013, when I first told a close friend I was writing a science fiction book at the age of 60. David, who is about 15 years younger than me and is always dressed in some type of blue shirt and blue jeans, just sat there, looking at me, for about 30 seconds. Then, he finally said, "I think that's great. It just goes to show you that it's never too late to chase your dreams."

I thought for a minute, wondering why he had waited to respond to me, and I said, "Thanks, David, you are right. It's never too late to do something you love. So, tell me, what are some of your dreams that you have put on hold?"

Now David was standing, staring out of the window, as if he were looking for his dream. The sun was shining brightly, and he turned away from it, as if it hurt his eyes, and said, "I always wanted to have my own fishing boat that I could take out into the ocean and maybe be a guide for fishermen, maybe do fishing tours. But I've been afraid to pursue it—afraid I might fail."

"David, tell me what sparked this dream," I said.

"Well, when I was younger, I would go fishing in the ocean with my granddad, in his boat. Just being on the ocean, seeing nothing but water, the boat gently rocking back and forth, and the excitement of catching fish. Then, the thrill to see how happy my granddad was with the whole experience. I would like to give that to others," David said.

I could see the passion and happiness in David's face and knew this was something he loved to do. "David, I started writing for my own entertainment. It makes me happy to know I created something from my imagination. It's also exciting to me to think someone else might enjoy what I write. I never thought about getting rich. It's the satisfaction of what I accomplished and to know I gave someone a little enjoyment. If I never sell a single book, I'm not going to stop writing. Remember, I do this for me, first, because I love it," I said. "Why don't you buy the boat for yourself, for your enjoyment?" I suggested.

"Oh, I plan to this year," David said.

"Good, that's the first step. Then, maybe you could start taking people out to fish on the weekends. See how it goes. You don't have to just jump into it. If it doesn't work out, you lost nothing, and you can still enjoy fishing. If it does work out, then you can quit your job and do the fish tours full-time. What do you say?" I asked.

David's face lit up. "You are right, I want this, because I love the ocean and fishing, first. If the fishing tours happens, it will happen. If they don't, I will still have my fishing," David said. "Thanks, Claude, I needed that. I forgot why I wanted to do it. Because it's what I love to do," David added as he headed out of my office.

So, the moral of this Story Speak is, if you love your dream, don't stop chasing that dream.

> *"The greatness of a man is not in how much wealth he acquires, but in his integrity and his ability to affect those around him positively."*
> *--Bob Marley*

CHAPTER 10

HOW WE LOOK

I touched on this throughout this book, because it is important. It's not so much how you dress, however, that plays a major part in successfully communicating. You all have heard the saying, "dress with confidence", which means take a little pride in what you wear. It will boost your confidence and create some positive energy.

As I said earlier, you want to be comfortable in what you wear. If you are not, that's a negative, and will take away your confidence and positive energy. Always keep this message in your mind as you prepare your day.

This chapter is going to cover how you handle yourself as you move through the day communicating. We have talked about body language, and how it can affect your communication with others, but what about the times when you are in meetings or in a group of friends? How do you handle yourself?

In the next few pages, we are going to cover several scenarios that can keep the positive energy flowing with just the way you handle your expressions and body language while hanging out.

Don't forget your body language: You still want to project confidence and openness with the others you are around. Good posture is a good start—it's positive and confident. If you show a slumping posture—or what I call a lazy one— that is definitely negative, and the ones around you will feed off your negativity.

Watch how you handle your arms and legs. Don't cross your arms. Keep your hands by your side or hold them in front of you. If you are sitting, put them in your lap. It's okay to change positions, so maybe sit a little sideways and put your arm across the back of the chair. The main thing is: no crossing your arms or put your hands in your pockets.

If you are standing, your legs and feet should be facing the group. This shows you are part of the group and conversation. If you are sitting, keep both feet on the floor, or cross your legs with one foot on your knee.

Review other things about body language, and see if other things will help you show the group you are a positive, supportive member of the group, even if you are not participating in the conversation.

Be attentive: Paying attention to the others you are with is not only respectful, but can also help others be confident through the positive support. I know you remember a time you were talking to others, and you noticed one person looking around. That affected you. It bothered you. In other words, it had a negative effect on you.

If the conversation is boring to you for some reason, you might be able to join in and direct it towards another topic. If that's not a possibility, then start thinking about the positive thing each member of the group project has and how it affects you. This will keep your thoughts in a positive mode.

Stay off your phone: Yes, stay off your phone. Turn it off if you can't resist looking at new notifications, emails, texts, or calls. Yes, seeing someone using their phone during a conversation is not only very distracting, but it is also very rude and creates a very negative atmosphere.

If you are someone who is required to be on-call and accessible at certain times, let the group know this is your call day in advance. This simple action helps keep everything positive if you happen to get a call or need to leave—but keep it on vibrate and step away from the group to take a call.

For those who have children—as all parents know—they will call or text you, and always at the wrong time. If it's an emergency, you should set up a code with your children. This way, all you need is a quick glance to see if it's an emergency, or something that can wait a little while. Hopefully, this will not distract the others.

It's better to engage than sit on the side. We may not realize it at first, that the conversation is something you want to be part of, but, after listening for a little while, you might find a benefit to join the conversation.

This doesn't necessarily mean you need to put your two-cents in, but a comment or agreement from time-to-time will not only help you stay positive, focused, and part of the group, it will probably make the others more comfortable— and that's another positive.

Being a silent member of the group is not a negative thing. It's okay to be silent, but remember, you are seen, and you still want to show respect, be supported, and show all positive body signs.

If you are attending a meeting and want to remember what was said for later, take notes— even if someone else is taking the minutes of the meeting. This is a good habit to pick up. Not only are you engaged, but sometimes this will make others feel like what they say is important. A positive. Plus, your notes are instantly ready for your use. You might have to wait for the minutes from the meeting for two or three days, and they may not be as detailed as your own notes.

If you are being lectured or in a training with a group, be seen. This may not seem like a big deal to some of you, but it's important to the one doing the lecture or training. Being a speaker and a trainer, we rely on how you are reacting to what we say. If I can't see you, I don't know if I'm conveying my message well or not.

Another reason for this is it sends a positive message that you are interested in what is going on. Believe it or not, if someone is behind someone, and you can't see their face, then you start to wonder if they are hiding, which is a distraction.

It doesn't matter where we are, or what we are doing—we have the opportunity to bring positivity to the table. Even if we are just hanging out with family and friends and taking it easy, it is easy to be commonly courteous and get someone an iced tea or a pillow, just to bring in some positivity.

Play a game with your children, let them win, or let your kids just have fun with the water hose in the summertime. Let someone watch the movie they like on TV, or play the music they like on the radio. These are all positive actions that are not hard to do.

Of course, boosting people's confidence is easy to do. Telling someone they are really good at something, talking to someone, looking them in the eyes, using their name several times, will all start that wave of positive energy in them.

We all have the tools to do this. It's easy and helps you keep the wave of positive energy flowing in you. It's important to always be consistent in your behavior.

> *"Develop our capacity to respond fully to all of life. Every action generates positive energy, which can be shared with others. These qualities of caring and responsiveness are the greatest gift we can offer." -* **Tarthang Tulku**

> *"A strong positive mental attitude will create more miracles than any wonder drug." -* **Patricia Neal**

CHAPTER 11

THE UNSHAKABLE

Throughout your life and your career, you are going to run across a few people who have so much negative energy and resist any positive energy. No matter what you do, it doesn't seem you can change their energy.

I like to call these "The Unshakable". These people will be very challenging to deal with, and sometimes, you just can't. Some people may have anger built up inside of them, or they just find problems with everything.

You have seen them at work, or even in your family. You may try to get to the root of the problem, but they resist that, too. Most of us are not psychologists, and we have to handle what we can.

There are a few things we can do that might let a little positive energy in. We want to avoid any conflicts or arguments, if possible, which means we need to be in control at all times, keeping the tone of our voice calm and consistent.

Sit down with them, so you are on the same level. This not only should make them feel a little more comfortable, as they don't get the feeling you are trying to dominate them.

If this is your child, younger family member, or younger friend, sit where they are comfortable—which might be the floor, bed, couch, etc. For a young person, it's important they feel they have a little control. It's different for an adult. You need to keep control in those situations.

Sitting at the same level usually builds trust and creates a bond. This may not work with an Unshakable, but it might. It harder to leave a conversation if you are sitting down than if you are standing. Also, it's easier to study their body language up close, which might help you in your conversation with them. You are looking for clues, or cues to see if anything you are saying is affecting them.

If they stand up like they are going to leave, you stand up and ask them to please sit down, so you two can finish the conversation. Never let them have the dominant position. You need to be the one in control—at all times. They may, or may not, sit back down. If not, their negative energy is still strong.

Make as much eye contact as possible. A lot of times, these folks will avoid eye contact, because they subconsciously know once eye contact is made, they will lose a little control, and the feeling is uncomfortable.

We all know that eye contact is positive and usually makes the other party feel like you like them. Unshakables don't want that. So, during a conversation with them, and when an opportunity happens, look them in the eyes.

Just remember, they will avoid eye contact as much as possible. So, don't worry about overdoing it when you do get to look at them eye-to-eye. Be sure you have your positive face on during the conversation. The last thing you want to do is put off any negative energy.

If you get to look into their eyes for three to four seconds, it also means you have their attention for that same amount of time. Try to make the best of it. If you get the chance to make eye contact four or five times during a 10-minute conversation, I think you are making progress.

Allow them to talk as much as possible. The more they talk, the more they are letting negative energy out. It also makes them feel they are in control. Sometimes, the more they talk, the more their own subconscious is re-evaluating their thoughts and could help reduce their negative energy.

As always, you want to listen to everything they say. They may say something that will trigger a positive response after they are finished talking. Waiting is not only a good courtesy, but you will have a better chance of having a positive impact.

Not everyone will want to talk. Be patient. You are trying to have the conversation because there is some type of problem. Don't pressure them to talk. You could ask for some help. You could say you acknowledge they may have a problem with the way you do things, and then ask the question, "Do you have a suggestion for a better solution?" or say, "Tell me what I can do better."

That shows trust and is a positive thing to do. It might get them to talk about the problem. If you are not sure what the problem is, start with some general questions to break the ice—like: Are you comfortable? Do you need something to drink?

If you are talking to a child, you may want to ask about their favorite sports, or their favorite activities—just something to get a few words started, and then maybe they will open up.

Some may never open up. Let them know you are there to talk when they are ready. Be sure to thank them for their time. Be appreciative. You can also try and have the conversation again later.

Be sure to follow up. If you feel you made some headway, relieved some of the negative energy, or gave them some positive energy, you should continue to help them and try to keep a positive atmosphere out there. If you are dealing with someone at work, this is a way to see they are improving and not affecting the rest of the team negatively.

Following-up shows your compassion and empathy, which shows your concern for their well-being and is positive. This may still be a work in progress, but progress is what you are looking for. Don't give up too soon.

In some cases, the follow-up may need to be done in a subtle way. The last thing you want to do is lose the trust you built. You may just want them to know they are doing well, or have another party evaluate them.

If it's a family member, the same rules apply— unless it's a child. If you have made some progress with them, you should be the one following up and continuing where you left off. The direct approach will work best, but don't be too forceful.

Sometimes, if the problem involves you, it might be better to let someone else try and handle the problem. If it is a family member or a friend, this could be the best option—at least, to start.

We can't always influence someone in a positive way, especially if you are part of the problem. Even if you are not part of the problem, it might be better to pass the buck if you haven't made any headway after you first conversation.

It is very simple: you may not be the person who can remove the negative energy or help to create a positive balance. There is always the chance the second person won't be able to help. They may do more damage. This is why most companies have Human Resources departments, and why families can find family counselors in their community or their church.

It's always disappointing to know you can't help everyone, but you must protect your own balance and keep your positive energy up. These cases are rare, and far between. Remember, if you help spread positive energy to five to ten people, you are helping to affect hundreds of people.

I only added this chapter so you know there will be people who are resistant to any positive attitudes. Some of them would prefer to try and take you down and try to fill you full of their negative energy. When it's possible, stay away from these types of people. Don't let them influence you.

> *"Even if you cannot change all the people around you, you can change the people you choose to be around. Life is too short to waste your time on people who don't respect, appreciate, and value you. Spend your life with people who make you smile, laugh, and feel loved." – **Roy T. Bennett***

"You cannot control what happens to you, but you can control the way you think about all the events. You always have a choice. You can choose to face them with a positive mental attitude."
– Roy T. Bennett

CHAPTER 11

RECAP

We have covered a lot of areas in communication—like what to do from the time you wake up, to dealing with your day. These suggestions and tools should help you develop a life of positive energy. The more you practice, the more rewards you will receive.

Being the Force of Positivity is a way of life. Once you start this journey, your life changes for the better, and you will never turn back to your old life.

We covered how important it was for us to talk to the whole person: the mind, body, and spirit. We sometimes only talk to the physical person and not the other two-thirds— the mind and emotions.

Let's recap a little:

We started out talking about how communication is general, and how failures to communicate create most of the problems we face. We covered the four causes of most of the failures:

1. Not listening.
2. Not enough details.
3. Not talking on the level of our audience.
4. Not enough information or facts.

We covered ways to avoid these problems and improve our communication skills in more positive ways.

Then, we discussed how important it is to start your day with a positive attitude and covered some suggestions to help. Remember, positivity starts at home, before you ever walk out the door.

1. Make your bed.
2. Get ready: brush your teeth, comb your hair, shave, put on makeup, get dressed, etc.
3. Smile at yourself.
4. Get enough rest.
5. Get your blood flowing.
6. Mediate or pray.

These are all good and positive things to set that wave of positive energy flowing in your subconscious before you start your day. After these, you have prepared for your day, and you are ready to share positive energy with others.

We covered how the subconscious works, and how words and phrases can have a positive effect on it—if they are used correctly. Endorphins are made in the subconscious, and we want to stimulate them to create that positive wave. We also covered how negative statements eliminate any positive efforts.

Certain words and phrases can build trust and form bond. Using someone's name makes them feel like you like them, and it's also important to ask permission. We suggested several positive words and phrases to use in a conversation, and using small talk makes you more accessible.

We discussed what not to say— such as asking for "big favors". You should never demand anything. I mentioned the importance of admitting you are wrong and when to realize you are part of a problem to show how you must show empathy and compassion when communicating.

Communicating with family and friends is different than communicating with co-works, supervisors, strangers, or acquaintances. It is important to be accessible to your family and friends by being a good listener and watching your own body language. It is also important to always be positive and communicate at your children's levels.

This book gives you skills to use, like style changes, confidence, friendliness, and learning body awareness. I also tried to encourage you to practice your communication skills and look for feedback and criticism, so you can improve your skills

We discussed body language from your head to your feet, like what to watch for when communicating with someone, how to position yourself during a conversation, and how certain actions can be positive or negative.

I told you about the art of telling stories to help make a point and get people's attention, and how stories have been used since the beginning of time to inspire, rally, and fire-up imaginations. The story needs to speak to these three elements: audio, visual, and emotional. Each story should be related to your subject and have a catch, a message, a solution, and a moral.

I mentioned that when you are in groups of people, you should care about how you look, what you wear, how you use your body language, how to be present and attentive, using common courtesy and respect, and how to be positive.

Lastly, we covered the "Unshakables"—the people who have a lot of negative energy for little reason. We shared different ways that you may be able help release some of their negativity, but sometimes you just need to let go and stay away from the Unshakable.

"Thought Talk" comes down to starting your day right, learning good ways to communicate positively—verbally and non-verbally—taking two seconds to wait for your subconscious, and understanding the other person's mind, body, and emotions, and communicating with the total person.

This recap is only two-and-a-half pages. When you read this, my intent was you would want to go back to certain areas of the book and re-read it for more details. You can tell from the recap that there is a lot of information in this book for you to use, and most of it is easy to do—once you get in the habit of using your skills.

Here's a list of helpful observations you can use anytime with your skills:

1. During an introduction, make a note of someone's eye color. You're not going to use the information—unless you plan to write them a poem—it's just a technique to achieve the optimum amount of eye contact, which people find friendly and confident.

2. People always have the clearest memory of the first and last things that happen, while the middle becomes a vague blur. So, as a leader, you want to ask if your instructions are clear, or ask for them to repeat them. If you bring up something in the middle of a meeting, you might want to repeat it the end of the meeting—during recap period. If you're setting the time for an interview, try and be the first or last through the door.

3. People's feet are often an insight into what they're thinking. For example, if you approach two people talking, and they turn their torso to you, but not their feet, they'd prefer you left them alone. Similarly, if you're talking to someone, and their feet are pointing away from you, they want to escape.

4. When laughter breaks out in a group of people, each one will instinctively glance at whichever other individual they feel closest to in that group. This might be a way to see who your allies or your enemies are. This is also a good way of spotting who is secretly sleeping together at work.

5. Like all therapists worth their fee, remember to use the power of silence. If someone gives you an unsatisfactory answer to a question, stay quiet and keep eye contact, and they'll usually feel pressured to keep talking and reveal more.

6. If you know someone is going to have a go at you in a meeting, deliberately sit right next to them. The proximity and mirrored direction of your bodies will make them feel less comfortable with

being aggressive, and you'll have an easier time of it.

7. Mirroring people's body language when you interact with them is a way of building up trust. Just be subtle about it.

8. When walking through a crowd, keep your gaze on the gaps between people, rather than the people, themselves. Usually, they'll part ways to let you through, meaning less West Side Story moments on Oxford Street.

9. A date that involves adrenaline – rollercoasters, horror films, etc. – will help simulate arousal in the brain and make people think they're enjoying your company, which hopefully they will be anyway.

10. A warm handshake makes you far more attractive to people than a cold one. The lesson here? Invest in some gloves.

11. The best way to learn is to teach. If you're acquiring a new skill or piece of knowledge, bore someone else with it at the first opportunity you get.

12. Finally, there is nothing more important to people than their self-image. Figure out how people like to think of themselves and challenge or reinforce it to your advantage.

As with all of these, please use responsibly.

Being a Force of Positivity becomes a way of life. You should always be consistent in your positive communication. There isn't anything more rewarding than knowing you affected someone life in a positive way and knowing they are going to affect someone else.

"As you practice and start communicating in positively, you will also be teaching others to do the same. Be that role model and help start the change." -- C. **Ray Collins.**

"A positive attitude gives you power over your circumstances, instead of your circumstances having power over you."
  –*Joyce Meyer*

REFERENCES AND ACKNOWLEDGEMENTS

References:

Stanford University Research - 1998

University of Missouri Research - Social Communication

University of Massachusetts – Micro Training

University of Massachusetts Medical School – Story telling and Health

Nicholas Boothman – Story Speak

Acknowledgements:

Dale Carnegie

Robin Roberts

Nicholas Boothman

John Fuller

Professor Alan Ivey

Dr Thomas Houston

QUOTES

Patrick Rothfess – page 5

Og Mandino – Page 14

Germany Kent – Page 24 & 48

Daniel Gomez – Page 29

Alec Stern – Page 29

Roy Bennett – Page 36, 53. 89 & 90

Zig Zigler – Page 40

Lisa Cypers Karmen – Page 40

Nicholas Boothman – Page 75 & 81

Bob Marley – Page 78

Tarthang Tulku – Page 83

Patricia Neal – Page 83

Joyce Meyers – Page 97

It's rare you run across a book that gives practical tools for the CEO and middle manager. When you do, you buy 3 copies. One to read for yourself, one to pass up to your boss and one to pass down to your team; this is that kind of book.

CRayCollins.com

Just 50 years from now, they will be the first! Ray Holland and a small group of professionals with unique backgrounds embark on the ultimate journey. They must travel through a wormhole to reach another world... only to find very human like beings with a similar history to Earth's!

CRayCollins.com

www.ingramcontent.com/pod-product-compliance
Lightning Source LLC
LaVergne TN
LVHW021333080526
838202LV00003B/156